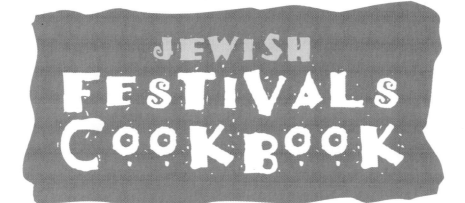

JEWISH FESTIVALS COOKBOOK

RONNE RANDALL
WITH PHOTOGRAPHY BY ZUL MUKHIDA

HODDER
Wayland

An imprint of Hodder Children's Books

FESTIVALS COOKBOOKS

CHRISTIAN FESTIVALS COOKBOOK

HINDU FESTIVALS COOKBOOK

JEWISH FESTIVALS COOKBOOK

CHINESE FESTIVALS COOKBOOK

© 2000 White-Thomson Publishing Ltd

Produced for Hodder Wayland by Margot Richardson
23 Hanover Terrace, Brighton, E Sussex, BN2 2SN, UK

Food photography: Zul Mukhida, Chapel Studios, Brighton
Design and illustrations: Tim Mayer
Proofreader: Philippa Smith

Published in Great Britain in 2000 by Hodder Wayland,
an imprint of Hodder Children's Books

The right of Ronne Randall to be identified as the author of this
Work has been asserted by her in accordance with the Copyright,
Designs and Patents Act 1988.

A catalogue record for this book is available from the British Library.

ISBN 0 7502 2634 X

Printed and bound by G. Canale & C.S.p.A., Turin

Photograph acknowledgements:
Art Directors and TRIP 5, (A Tovy), 15 (Muzlish); Eye Ubiquitous 23 (Kevin
Nicol); The Hutchison Library 13 (Liba Taylor); Impact Photos 4 (Robin
Laurance); Panos Pictures 21 (A S Guelon), 29 (N Durrell-McKenna); The
Stockmarket 6 (Paul), 7, 14, 22.

Hodder Children's Books
A division of Hodder Headline
338 Euston Road, London NW1 3BH

CONTENTS

JUDAISM AND ITS FOOD

The Jewish religion – Judaism – dates back to the time of Abraham in the Bible: about 1800 BC. At that time, the Jewish people lived in the Middle East, in the land that is now known as Israel. Today, Israel is once again a Jewish homeland, but Jewish people now live all over the world, in many different kinds of communities.

Most Jews today call themselves either Ashkenazim (those who have their origins in Germany and eastern Europe) or Sephardim (those whose roots are in Spain, North Africa, the Middle East or Asia).

All the different groups celebrate the same festivals, but many of their customs and traditions are different – including many of their traditional foods.

Jewish people are found all over the world. These boys live in the USA.

SaFeTY anD HYGiene

When cutting with knives, frying, boiling and using the oven, ALWAYS ask an adult to help you.

Food must always be kept clean. Food that gets dirty will not taste good – and can even make people sick.

Always wash your hands before you start cooking.

Do not wipe dirty hands on a towel. Wash your hands first.

If you need to taste something while cooking, use a clean fork or spoon.

Make sure work surfaces are clean and dry. This includes tables, worktops and chopping boards.

Jews came from many countries to settle in Israel. These girls are celebrating the country's 50th anniversary.

All Jews have religious laws that tell them what they may or may not eat. These laws come from the Torah, the Jewish holy book, which was given to Moses on Mount Sinai.

They forbid the eating of all pig meat as well as some other meats, such as rabbit. Shellfish is also forbidden, and meat and dairy products may not be cooked or eaten together. Food that Jews are permitted to eat is called kosher, which means 'proper' or 'correct'.

ROSH HASHANAH

The Jewish calendar is based on the cycles of the moon. There are twelve months. Each one begins with the new moon, and lasts 29 or 30 days. The first month is Tishri, which falls in late summer or early autumn. This is when Rosh Hashanah, the festival of the New Year, is celebrated.

Rosh Hashanah marks the creation of the world, which, according to Jewish tradition, happened nearly 6,000 years ago. It is a time when Jews think about the year that has just passed, and look forward to being a better person in the year to come.

During prayers at the synagogue, the *shofar*, a ram's horn, is sounded. The loud, piercing blast of the *shofar* is a kind of 'wake-up call' to remind everyone to pay more attention to God's laws. Over the next ten days, people apologize to anyone they have wronged over the past year, and ask God's forgiveness for their sins. This solemn period finishes with Yom Kippur, the Day of Atonement, when Jews fast and say prayers of repentance.

Blowing the *shofar* at Rosh Hashanah.

6

On Rosh Hashanah, however, everyone is happy and looking forward to the coming year. People send New Year's cards, and exchange the traditional greeting: '*L'shanah tova tikatavu*': 'May you be inscribed for a good year.' Festive meals begin with apples and challah (a type of bread) dipped in honey. They also include other sweet foods, to symbolize hopes for a sweet and happy year.

Rosh Hashanah meals always begin with sweet foods, such as apples and honey. The typical round challah (see pages 8–9) is also on the table.

Round Challah

Preparation time: 3 hours

Cooking time: 45–55 minutes

Oven Temperature: 200 °C/ Gas Mark 6

Serves: 8–10

Ingredients

450 g strong white flour

1¹/₂ tsp salt

7 g dry yeast ('easy bake'/ 'easy blend')

75 g raisins

2 eggs

250 ml warm water

2 tbsp vegetable oil

2 tbsp sugar

Oil for greasing

1 egg yolk

1 tsp cold water

Equipment

3 large mixing bowls

Wooden spoons

Tea-towel

Baking tray

Pastry brush

This special, slightly sweet bread (pronounced 'hal-lah') is eaten at the Sabbath and at most festival meals. Usually the loaf is plaited, but at Rosh Hashanah the challah is round, to symbolize the cycle of the year. (The round shape also looks something like a crown, as a reminder that God is king.) Sometimes raisins are added, to bring extra sweetness to the coming year.

1 Put the flour and the salt into a large mixing bowl. Add the yeast and raisins and mix well. Make a well in the centre of the mixture.

2 In another large bowl, beat the two eggs. Add the water, oil and sugar. Mix well.

3 Add the liquid to the bowl of flour and beat together until a ball of dough forms.

4 Turn out the dough on to a lightly floured surface and knead well, for about 5 minutes. Then put it into a lightly greased bowl, cover with a clean tea-towel and let it rise for about 2 hours. The dough should double in size.

5 When the dough has risen, knead it again and roll it into a rope about 2 cm thick.

6 Coil it from the outside in, letting each circle slightly overlap the one before. Place the loaf on a greased baking tray and let it rise for 25 minutes. With an adult's help, pre-heat the oven.

7 Mix the egg yolk and the cold water, and brush over the whole challah. Bake for 10–15 minutes. Then lower the heat to 180 °C/Gas Mark 4 and bake for another 35–40 minutes.

Apple and Honey Cake

Preparation time: 30 minutes

Cooking time: 45 minutes

Oven temperature: 180 °C/ Gas Mark 4

Serves: 8–10

Ingredients

2 medium dessert apples

4 tbsp vegetable oil

225 g honey

2 eggs

225 g self-raising flour

$\frac{1}{2}$ tsp salt

1 tsp ground cinnamon

$\frac{1}{2}$ tsp ground ginger

$\frac{1}{2}$ tsp ground nutmeg

Equipment

2-pound (1.5 litre) loaf tin

Greaseproof paper

Vegetable peeler

Chopping knife

Large mixing bowl

Wooden spoon

Sieve

Cocktail stick

Wire rack

Honey is the traditional Rosh Hashanah food, and it is eaten in many dishes over the New Year period. The main festival meal would not be complete without a moist and chewy honey cake for dessert. This spicy cake also uses apples, another special Rosh Hashanah food, for double sweetness. Serve plain or drizzled with more honey for a super-sweet New Year!

1 Ask an adult to help you pre-heat the oven. Grease the loaf tin and line with greaseproof paper.

2 Peel, core and chop the apples.

3 Mix the oil with the honey, then mix in the eggs.

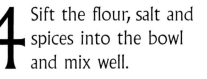

4 Sift the flour, salt and spices into the bowl and mix well.

5 Add the apple pieces and stir.

6 Pour the mixture into the tin and, with an adult's help, bake for about 45 minutes.

7 The cake is done when it is golden brown on top and a cocktail stick inserted in the centre comes out clean. Cool in the tin for 5 minutes, then turn out on to a wire rack.

Carrot Tzimmes

A tzimmes is a kind of sweet stew made with fruits or vegetables, and sometimes with meat, that is very popular among Ashkenazi Jews, especially at the Sabbath and festivals. Carrot tzimmes has always been a Rosh Hashanah favourite, perhaps because the carrots look like gold coins when they are sliced into rounds, symbolizing prosperity and good luck.

Preparation time: 10 minutes

Cooking time: 45 minutes

Serves: 6–8

Ingredients

750 g carrots

3 tbsp vegetable oil

1/2 tsp salt

75 ml orange juice

1 tsp cinnamon

2 tbsp honey

Equipment

Vegetable peeler

Chopping knife

Wide saucepan

Wooden spoon

1 Scrape or peel the carrots, then ask an adult to help you slice them into rounds about 5 mm thick.

2 With an adult's help, heat the oil in a wide saucepan. Add the carrots and cook gently for 2–3 minutes. Turn them over once or twice so they heat through evenly.

3 Add the salt, orange juice, cinnamon and honey. Add just enough water to cover.

4 Ask an adult to bring everything to the boil. Then lower the heat and simmer gently, covered, for about 20 minutes.

5 Remove the lid of the pan and continue to simmer gently until the carrots are tender and glazed.

OTHER ROSH HASHANAH TRADITIONS

A popular custom among Jews the world over is to eat a new fruit of the season for the first time at Rosh Hashanah. In Israel, this is often the pomegranate because they are said to have 613 seeds, the same as the number of commandments given to Jews in the Torah.

In some Sephardi communities it is traditional to eat dishes made with black-eyed peas at the New Year. In Aramaic, the language that was spoken in much of the ancient Middle East, the word for black-eyed peas, *rubiya*, also meant 'wealth'. Therefore, eating *rubiya* at Rosh Hashanah would bring riches in the coming year.

Passing a plate of pomegranate pieces at a family Rosh Hashanah dinner.

Another popular custom in some Sephardi families is to serve a whole fish for the main course of the Rosh Hashanah meal. The fish's head is left on when it is brought to the table, to symbolize leadership and looking forward. When the fish is first tasted, an old tradition is that everyone at the table should say: 'In the coming year, may we be leaders; may we be the head, and not the tail.'

Passover

Passover is the spring festival of freedom. Called *Pesach* in Hebrew, it is one of the most joyous of all Jewish festivals. It celebrates the Jews' escape from slavery in Egypt more than 3,000 years ago; it is also a festival of spring and new life.

During the eight days of Passover, matzah, a flat, unleavened bread, is eaten instead of ordinary bread. No foods with leavening (the ingredient that makes dough rise) are permitted. In the days leading up to Passover, Jewish homes are cleaned thoroughly. Every crumb is swept out of cupboards and shelves, and all leavened foods are put away.

The highlight of the Passover celebration is the *seder*, the special meal that takes place on the first two nights of the festival. *Seder* means 'order' in Hebrew, and the meal does follow a set order.

At the *seder* meal, the senior member of the family blesses the matzah. The symbolic foods (see page 15) can be seen on baskets at each end of the table.

Symbolic foods on the *seder* plate include

● a bitter herb such as horseradish, to remind Jews of the bitterness of slavery.

● salt water, as a reminder of the tears the Jews shed.

● a green vegetable such as lettuce or parsley, as a symbol of life and springtime.

● *charoseth*, a mixture of apples, nuts, wine, and cinnamon, as a reminder of the mortar used by the Jewish slaves when they built cities for the Egyptians.

● a roasted egg and bone to symbolize the Passover sacrifice brought to the Temple in Jerusalem in ancient times.

During the *seder*, the youngest person at the table recites four questions from the *Hagadah*.

After candles are lit and blessings are said, the youngest child at the table asks four questions, beginning with: 'Why is this night different from all other nights?' In reply, the person leading the *seder* reads the story of the escape from Egypt from a book called a *Hagadah*. Symbolic foods are set out on a special *seder* plate, and four cups of wine are drunk at specific times during the meal. A special cup of wine is placed on the table for the Prophet Elijah who, according to legend, visits every Jewish home on Passover.

During the *seder*, the leader hides the *afikomen*, a special piece of matzah that is to be eaten at the end of the meal. All the children search for it, and the child who finds it can bargain for a reward (usually sweets), because the *seder* cannot be finished without it! Some people keep a piece of the *afikomen* in a pocket or drawer, to bring them good luck throughout the coming year.

Matzah

Preparation time: 20 minutes

Cooking time: 5 minutes

Oven temperature:
240 °C/Gas Mark 9

Makes: 6 matzahs

Ingredients

250 g plain flour

150 ml cold water

Oil for greasing

Equipment

Large mixing bowl

Wooden spoon

Rolling pin

Large baking tray

Fork

Matzah is the unleavened bread that is eaten at Passover. It reminds Jews today that their ancestors left Egypt in a great hurry, and didn't have time to let their bread dough rise. Instead, they let the dough bake in the sun as they began their journey across the desert to the promised land of Israel. Many supermarkets nowadays sell matzah, but it is quick, easy and fun to make your own.

1 Pre-heat the oven. This is a very hot oven, so make sure an adult is there to help you. In a large mixing bowl, combine the flour and the water. Mix well.

2 Knead the mixture into a firm dough.

3 Divide the dough into 5 cm-diameter balls.

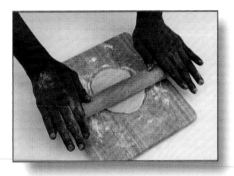

4 On a clean surface, flatten each ball with your hand, then roll out into the thinnest sheets possible (no more than about 5 mm). Each ball should make an oval sheet about 14 x 17 cm.

5 Oil the baking tray. Transfer the sheets to the tray. Prick each sheet with a fork in parallel lines about 1 cm apart.

6 Bake for 3–5 minutes, or until crisp and beginning to turn brown. Let the matzahs cool completely before eating. They will become crisper as they cool.

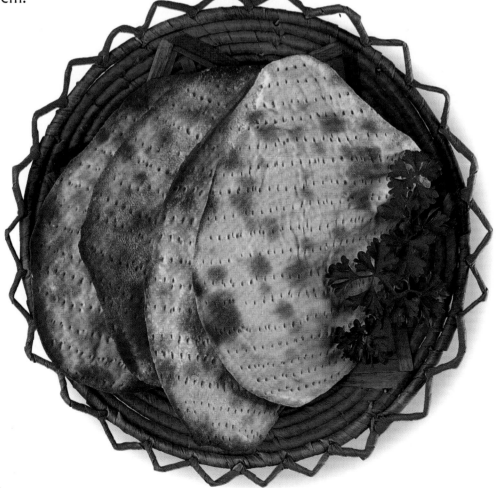

Spinach Frittata

Preparation time: 20 minutes

Cooking time: 10 minutes

Serves: 6-8

Ingredients

300 g frozen spinach, thawed

3 matzahs

4 eggs

$1/2$ tsp salt

Pinch of ground nutmeg

3 tbsp butter or margarine

Parmesan cheese, grated

Equipment

Sieve or colander

Two mixing bowls

Wooden spoon

Frying pan

Egg slice

Matzah is, of course, eaten on its own during Passover, instead of bread. But it is also used as an ingredient in many dishes, often in the form of finely ground matzah meal, instead of ordinary flour.

These firm, pancake-like omelettes are popular with Sephardi Jews; Ashkenazi Jews make a similar dish called *Matzah Brei*.

1 Drain the spinach as thoroughly as you can, and reserve half the liquid.

2 Crumble the matzahs into a different bowl. Add the spinach and pour the reserved liquid over them. Mix thoroughly until the matzahs are soft.

3 Beat the eggs, then add to the spinach mixture. Add the salt and nutmeg. Mix well.

4 With an adult's help, melt the butter or margarine in a frying pan and add the spinach and matzah mixture. Cook on medium heat for about 5 minutes each side, until firm and browned.

5 Sprinkle with grated Parmesan and serve immediately.

Coconut Pyramids

Preparation time: 30 minutes

Cooking time: 15 minutes

Oven temperature:
190 °C/Gas Mark 5

Makes: 12 pyramids

Ingredients

Vegetable oil

225 g dried unsweetened coconut

140 g caster sugar

2 eggs, beaten

Equipment

Baking tray

Brush for oil

Mixing bowl

Wooden spoon

Spatula

Ordinary biscuits and cakes are not eaten during Passover, but there is no shortage of festive treats! Passover sweets are made with ingredients such as very finely ground matzah meal, ground nuts, or coconut, like these sweet and chewy treats. The pyramid shape of these sweets is a reminder of the pyramids that the Jewish slaves helped to build in Egypt.

1 Ask an adult to help you pre-heat the oven. Grease the baking tray with a little vegetable oil.

2 Put all the ingredients into the mixing bowl. Mix together thoroughly, so they form a paste.

3 Form the mixture into little four-sided pyramids, about 5 cm square. It helps to wet your hands with cold water, so the mixture doesn't stick.

4 Using the spatula, place the pyramids on the baking tray. Bake until lightly golden-brown (about 15 minutes).

OTHER PASSOVER TRADITIONS

Ashkenazi and Sephardi Jews have some different Passover food traditions. Sephardim eat rice, pulses, beans and sweetcorn; Ashkenazi Jews do not, as they consider these foods too similar to grains, which are forbidden (wheat is allowed only for making matzah.) This is because there is a chance that these foods might ferment, as yeast does when it makes bread dough rise.

Many Sephardi Jews have lamb as the main course at the *seder* meal, and others serve stuffed lamb intestines during the Passover week.

Both groups have a variety of sweet treats, including cakes made with cinnamon, coconut or ground almonds.

At the end of Passover, Moroccan Jews hold a final celebration called the Mimouna, a time of merry-making and rejoicing. There is another festival meal, set out on a table decorated with leaves and grasses, to symbolize springtime and the rebirth of nature. Traditionally, only sweet foods are eaten at this meal. In Israel, the Mimouna has become a national celebration, with picnics in the parks, carnivals and dancing in the streets.

Sephardi Jews include those from Ethiopia, in north Africa. Many Ethiopian Jews now live in Israel.

SHaVUot

Shavuot falls on the sixth day of the Hebrew month of Sivan. It marks the day when Moses is said to have received the Torah on Mount Sinai. Moses was the leader who helped to bring the Jews out of slavery in Egypt.

The Torah, also known as the Five Books of Moses, is the Jewish holy book, containing all the laws that form the basis of Jewish practices, including the Ten Commandments. Moses received the Torah seven weeks after the Jews left Egypt. Shavuot, therefore, always falls exactly seven weeks after Passover. In fact, the word Shavuot means 'weeks' in Hebrew.

Shavuot is also a harvest festival, and one of the three Pilgrim Festivals in the Jewish calendar. (The other two are Passover and Sukkot, an autumn festival.) More than 2,000 years ago, when the Holy Temple stood in Jerusalem, Jews made pilgrimages from many countries to celebrate these festivals at the Temple, and to bring offerings to God. At Shavuot, the first wheat crops were being harvested, so sheaves of wheat were brought as offerings.

Today, Shavuot, like all Jewish festivals, is celebrated in the synagogue and at home. In the synagogue, the Ten Commandments are read out from the Torah scroll. It is traditional for the congregation to stand to hear them, just as the ancient Jews stood at the foot of Mount Sinai. At home, families celebrate with festive meals made with milk, cheese and other dairy foods. This is because the Jews received the Torah when they were on their way to Israel, which the Bible calls 'a land flowing with milk and honey'.

Reading from the Torah scroll is an important part of worship in the synagogue. After the reading, the Torah may be held up and carried round the synagogue. In some communities, like this one in Jerusalem, it may even be paraded through the streets.

Cheese Blintzes

Blintzes – thin pancakes filled with fruit, cheese, or other fillings, and then fried or baked – are a favourite East European dish that Ashkenazi Jews have taken with them all over the world. Blintzes are often eaten as a sweet, but at Shavuot, cheese blintzes may be eaten as a light meal on their own. They are delicious served with yogurt or jam – or just by themselves.

Preparation: 30 minutes

Cooking time: 15 minutes

Oven temperature:
180 °C/Gas Mark 4

Makes: 6-8 blintzes

Ingredients

Pancakes

1 egg

120 ml milk

1/2 tsp salt

1 1/2 tsp vegetable oil

50 g plain flour

Filling

225 g cottage cheese

1 egg

1 tsp sugar

1/4 tsp vanilla essence

Oil for frying and greasing

Jam or fruit sauce

Equipment

2 mixing bowls

Fork

Spoons

Frying pan

Pastry brush

Tea-towel

Ovenproof dish

1 To make the pancake batter, mix the egg, milk, salt and oil. Beat together with a fork. Then add the flour and mix well until smooth and creamy.

2 Give the frying pan a light coating of oil and, with an adult's help, put it on a medium heat.

3 When the frying pan is very hot, pour a small amount of batter (about 2 tablespoons) into the pan and turn so the batter coats the bottom of the pan. Cook for about a minute, until the pancake is golden-brown on one side.

24

4 Turn the pancake out onto a tea-towel with the brown side up. Repeat until all the pancake batter is used up.

5 Make the filling by putting all the ingredients together in a bowl and mixing well.

6 Ask an adult to help you pre-heat the oven. Take a pancake, brown side up. Put about 1 tablespoon of filling at one end and roll it up. Fold the ends over the centre of the blintz to seal it.

7 Grease the oven dish. Carefully put the blintzes into the dish, sealed side down, and bake in the oven until they are golden-brown.

Mini Cheesecakes

For Ashkenazi Jews, no Shavuot festival meal is complete without cheesecake for dessert. Like blintzes, cheesecake originated in eastern Europe, but it is now enjoyed throughout the world in many different varieties. These simple little cheesecakes are easy to make – and lots of fun to eat.

Preparation time: 20 minutes

Cooking time: 25 minutes

Oven temperature: 170 °C/Gas Mark 3

Makes: 6 cheesecakes

Ingredients

3 digestive biscuits, crushed

200 g cream cheese, softened

50 g caster sugar

1/2 tsp vanilla essence

1 egg

Equipment

Muffin tin

Paper muffin cases

Rolling pin

Mixing bowl

Spoons

1 Ask an adult to help you to pre-heat the oven. Line the muffin tin with the paper muffin cases.

2 Crush the digestive biscuits with the rolling pin. Put about a tablespoon of biscuit crumbs in the bottom of each cup.

3 Mix the cream cheese, sugar and vanilla essence together until well blended. Then add the egg and mix well.

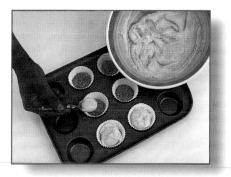

4 Spoon the cheese mixture into the muffin cups until they are almost full — but don't fill them all the way to the top.

5 Bake for about 25 minutes, until lightly golden on top and brown at the edges. Let the cheesecakes cool in the tin, then chill in the fridge. Serve cold.

Sweet Milk Pudding

Cooking time: 30 minutes

Serves: 6

Ingredients

50 g ground rice

50 g caster sugar

475 ml milk

$^1/_2$ tsp vanilla essence, or
$1^1/_2$ tsp rose water

Ground cinnamon

Equipment

Saucepan

Tablespoon

Wooden spoon

Among Sephardi Jews, milky puddings made with rice flour are the traditional dessert at Shavuot. This pudding is flavoured with vanilla in Turkey and the Balkans, and with rose water in Egypt and Syria. If you can find rose water in your supermarket, you might want to try it: it makes a very fragrant and unusual dessert. You can serve the pudding warm, or chill in the fridge and serve cold.

1 In the saucepan, mix the ground rice with the sugar.

2 Add a couple of tablespoons of milk and blend to make a smooth paste. Then gradually add the rest of the milk.

3 Over medium heat, bring the mixture to the boil, stirring gently all the time. Ask an adult to help you do this.

4 When the mixture boils, lower the heat and simmer until the mixture is thick and creamy (about 10 minutes). Keep stirring as the pudding thickens, to stop it sticking to the bottom of the pan.

5 Remove the pan from the heat and stir in the vanilla or rose water. Then pour the pudding into serving bowls and sprinkle cinnamon on top.

OTHER SHAVUOT TRADITIONS

Shavuot has several other names, including *Chag ha'Katzir* ('Festival of the Harvest'), because of the harvesting of the new wheat.

In Israel today, Shavuot is still celebrated as a harvest festival. On the group farms known as *kibbutzim*, wagons and tractors are decorated with flowers and loaded with newly harvested wheat and fruit. Children are given rides round the *kibbutz*, and everyone gathers for a party afterwards, where there is plenty of milk, along with sweet Shavuot treats.

In some places, the wheat harvest is remembered with special festival challahs for Shavuot. Ukrainian Jews, for example, bake challahs with a ladder design, to symbolize Moses climbing up Mount Sinai. The ladder has either five rungs (for the five Books of Moses) or seven rungs (for the number of weeks between Passover and Shavuot). In some Jewish communities in Greece, the Shavuot challah is made with yogurt and honey, and some German Jews bake a special cheese challah for Shavuot.

Traditional dancing is part of the celebrations at a *kibbutz* harvest festival in Israel.

FURTHER INFORMATION

When using the recipes contained in this book, children should be supervised by one or more adults at all times. This especially applies when cutting with knives, cooking on a cooker hob and using the oven.

Food and food traditions are central to Jewish life and an integral part of almost all Jewish celebrations. The festivals explored in this book are just three of about a dozen major and minor festivals that occur in the Jewish year. A few of the others with strong food associations are Sukkot, Hanukkah, Tu B'Shevat and Purim.

Sukkot, an autumn harvest festival, begins just five days after the solemn observance of Yom Kippur, and lasts for seven days.

Fruit and vegetable dishes are popular and, during Sukkot, meals are eaten in a *sukkah*, or booth – a temporary structure built as a reminder both of the temporary shelters the Jews lived in during the journey across the desert to the Promised Land, and of the huts farmers in Israel dwelt in during the harvest.

Hanukkah, the Festival of Lights, usually occurs in December, the darkest time of the year. It celebrates the Jews'

victory over the Greeks, and the rededication of the Holy Temple in Jerusalem. The *menorah* (holy lamp) in the temple had only enough oil to last one day and, according to legend, it miraculously lasted for eight days, until new oil could be made.

To mark this miracle, an eight-branched candlestick is lit at Hanukkah – one candle each night, until all eight are lit – and foods fried in oil are eaten, particularly potato pancakes (known as *latkes*), and jam doughnuts.

Tu B'Shevat, also known as the New Year for Trees, occurs in February, when the trees in Israel are just beginning to bear fruit.

It is celebrated by planting trees and eating fruits that grow on trees. Because it occurs on the fifteenth day of the month of Shevat, it is customary to eat fifteen different fruits, including one that has not yet been eaten so far that year.

Purim, which usually falls in March, is one of the most joyous days of the Jewish year.

It celebrates the time when Queen Esther, the Jewish wife of a Persian king, saved her people from death at the hands of the king's evil minister, Haman.

As part of the celebrations, Jews eat *hamantaschen*, or 'Haman's pockets', sweet triangular pastries filled with poppy seeds or fruit jam. It is also customary to exchange gifts of food with friends on Purim, and to give food to the poor and homeless.

COOKING METHODS

Round Challah: Please make sure that the dried yeast used in this recipe is the type that does not need reconstituting with water before adding to the other ingredients.

Sweet Milk Pudding: Ground rice is available in many shops, but if you can't find any, you can make your own by whizzing uncooked white rice in a blender or food processor until it is fine and powdery.

EQUIPMENT

The recipes in this book are written on the understanding that adults have access to weighing and measuring equipment, such as scales and measuring jugs.

TOPIC WEB

Science
Food and nutrition
Changing materials through heat
Separating/mixing of materials

English
Write a menu for a festive dinner
Traditional Jewish stories from
different countries

Geography
Location of Israel:
culture/landscape/climate, etc.
Jewish settlement around world

Maths
Using and understanding
data/measures/fractions
Using measuring instruments

JEWISH
FESTIVALS
COOKBOOK

History
Eastablishment of modern state
of Israel
Egypt under the Pharaohs

Design and Technology
Design a solar matzah baker
Design and make a moving
calendar: solar or lunar

RE
Jewish beliefs/worship/customs/
traditions/family/community
Biblical history

Modern Foreign Languages
Names/words re: festivals
Modern use of Hebrew and
Yiddish/crossover to English

GLOSSARY

Cycles Things that happen again and again in the same order. For example, each month the moon goes through the same pattern of changing shapes, from the new moon (when almost none of it is visible) through to the full moon, and back to the tiny sliver before the next new moon. Also called phases.

Fast Not eat; go without food, for a day, or for a longer time.

Ferment Change in a chemical way, converting sugars to alcohol and gas.

Homeland A country that is special to a particular group of people. They think of this land as their home, even if they were not born there.

Inscribed Written down in a special, formal way.

Meal Grain or matzah that has been ground very finely and can be used in cooking.

Mortar A thick mixture of cement, sand and water that is used to hold bricks or building stones together.

Pilgrim Festivals Three festivals (Passover, Shavuot and Sukkot) when, in ancient times, Jews made special trips to Jerusalem to celebrate.

Pomegranate A juicy, reddish fruit that contains many seeds. It is mentioned many times in the Bible.

Pyramids Ancient Egyptian monuments, with a rectangular base and four triangular sides, that held the tombs of Egyptian kings and other important people.

Sabbath The seventh day of creation, when God rested after making the world and everything in it. Jews celebrate the Sabbath on Saturday, keeping it as a day of rest and prayer.

Sacrifice Something given up to God, especially as part of a religious ceremony.

Sheaves Stalks of wheat, barley or other grain, tied into bundles. A single bundle is called a sheaf.

Slavery Being forced to work without getting any payment or reward. Slaves are owned by the people they work for.

Symbolize To stand for another object, or for an idea.

Synagogue A building where Jews come to pray and learn.

Ten Commandments The ten laws, written on two stone tablets, that God gave to Moses on Mount Sinai.

Traditions Things people do and believe, which are passed down over many generations.

Unleavened Baked without yeast or anything else that makes dough rise.

INDEX

Page numbers in **bold** refer to photographs

RESOURCES

Books
A Feast of Festivals, by Hugo Slim (Marshall Pickering, 1996)
A Flavour of Israel: Food and Festivals, by Ronne Randall (Wayland, 1999)
I Am a Jew, by Clive Lawton and Ilana Goldman (Franklin Watts, 1993)
Jewish Festivals, by Angela Wood (Heinemann, 1995)
Jewish Festival Tales by Saviour Pirotta (Hodder Wayland, 2000)
Judaism, by Sue Penny (Heinemann, 1997)
Looking at Judaism: Festivals, by Sharon Barron (Wayland, 1998)

A World of Festivals: Passover, by David Rose and Gill Rose (Evans Brothers Ltd, 1997)
World Religions: Judaism, by Angela Wood (Wayland, 1995)

Web sites
www.anjy.org
    Jewish youth web site with a variety of activities, including finding penfriends, Jewish resources and games.
www.jewmusm.ort.org
    Web site of London's Jewish museum: covers the life of Jewish people in Britain and beyond.